Book D

Who would have thought that the world would see such a day? With more fatalities and hospitalizations, COVID-19 has turned the world upside down for many. With schools being shut down, people working from home, public places closed and social distancing protocols in place, life isn't the same anymore.

How are we going to cope with the changing dynamics? What does the future ahead look like? How will parents make both ends meet? Will our children's education suffer?

All these are questions on the top of the mind of everyone. Some are worried about keeping their jobs while others mourn the death of a loved one.

Children have been hit by the pandemic too. They are missing out on some of the most important milestones in their lives and are pissed about it. So how can we, as their parents, help them handle the stress and uncertainty about things? How do we make them see the bright side of things and avoid going into depression fearing for their and their loved ones' lives?

In this unique and much-needed guide, Frank Dixon offers his readers an insight on how to help calm the anxiety many children and teenagers face today. With groundbreaking research, and scientific studies under scrutiny, he compiles seven essential methods to calm anxiety among kids and help them regulate negative emotions better. This is a guide for parents to help them find healthy ways to deal with this unexpected chain of events and continue to hope for the best amid these difficult times.

7 Effective Methods for Calming Kids Anxiety During the Covid-19 Pandemic

Easy Parenting Tips for Providing Your Kids Anxiety Relief and Preventing Teen Depression Caused by Coronavirus Isolation

Frank Dixon

professional advice. The content within this book has been derived from various sources. Please consult a licensed professional before attempting any techniques outlined in this book.

By reading this document, the reader agrees that under no circumstances is the author responsible for any losses, direct or indirect, that are incurred as a result of the use of the information contained within this document, including, but not limited to, errors, omissions, or inaccuracies.

OTHER BOOKS BY FRANK DIXON

How Parents Can Raise Resilient Children: Preparing Your Child for the Real Tough World of Adulthood by Instilling Them With Principles of Love, Self-Discipline, and Independent Thinking

❄ ❄ ❄

How Parents Can Teach Children To Counter Negative Thoughts: Channelling Your Child's Negativity, Self-Doubt and Anxiety Into Resilience, Willpower and Determination

❄ ❄ ❄

The Vital Parenting Skills and Happy Children Box Set: A 5 Full-Length Parenting Book Compilation for Raising Happy Kids Who Are Honest, Respectful and Well-Adjusted

❄ ❄ ❄

The 7 Vital Parenting Skills and Confident Kids Box Set: A 7 Full-Length Positive Parenting Book Compilation for Raising Well-Adjusted Children

❄ ❄ ❄

For a complete list, please visit http://bestparentingbooks.org/books

YOUR FREE GIFT

Before we begin, I have something special waiting for you. Another action-paced book, free of cost. Think of it as my way of saying thank you to you for purchasing this.

Your gift is a special PDF actionable guide titled, ***"Profoundly Positive Parenting: Learn the Top 10 Skills to Raising Extraordinary Kids!"***

As the title suggests, it's a collection of 10 parenting skills that will help you pave the way towards raising amazing and successful children. It's short enough to read quickly, but meaty enough to offer actionable advice that can make impactful changes to the way you parent.

Intrigued, I knew you would be!

Claim your copy of Profoundly Positive Parenting by clicking on the link below and join my mailing list:

http://bestparentingbooks.org/free-gift/

PROFOUNDLY
POSITIVE PARENTING

Learn the Top 10 Parenting Skills
to Raising Extraordinary Kids!

FRANK DIXON

Before we jump in, I'd like to express my gratitude. I know this mustn't be the first book you came across and yet you still decided to give it a read. There are numerous courses and guides you could have picked instead that promise to make you an ideal and well-rounded parent while raising your children to be the best they can be.

But for some reason, mine stood out from the rest and this makes me the happiest person on the planet right now. If you stick with it, I promise this will be a worthwhile read.

In the pages that follow, you're going to learn the best parenting skills so that your child can grow to become the best version of themselves and in doing so experience a meaningful understanding of what it means to be an effective parent.

Notable Quotes About Parenting

"Children Must Be Taught How To Think,
Not What To Think."

— Margaret Mead

"It's easier to build strong children than to fix
broken men [or women]."

- Frederick Douglass

"Truly great friends are hard to find, difficult
to leave, and impossible to forget."

— George Randolf

"Nothing in life is to be feared, it is only to be
understood. Now is the time to understand
more, so that we may fear less."

— Scientist Marie Curie

Table of Contents

Introduction

Who would have thought that we would see a day like this? A time when uncertainty walks the streets. A time when we would have to stay indoors for an unknown number of days, stuck with every other family member of the house. A time when all forms of movements would be restricted, and we need a solid reason to leave the house—all while wearing a mask and a pair of gloves. Yes, lockdowns can be scary. They are even scarier for our children who can't cope with the uncertainty. They are missing school, their friends, important milestones like prom and graduation, etc. They don't know when things will get back to normal or if they ever will.

As more and more countries restrict movement to reduce the number of COVID-19 cases, we are all left with nothing but to make some drastic changes to our lifestyles and routines.

The new reality where adults are bound to work from home and still worry about having a job at the end of this, and children missing social interactions and the casual hustle-bustle of the day, lack of physical contact from relatives, and spending public holidays and celebrations in the vicinity of our homes is strikingly unreal and depressing.

We are all living in constant fear of contracting the virus and what will happen if we don't make it. We are worried about our children, about our partners who have to go to the office a couple of days in the week and about the elders in the family who are the most susceptible to contracting it. Add to that, the effect all of this has on our and our children's mental and emotional health.

As parents, we have to watch out for our family. We have to ensure that we keep them safe. We have to abide by the safety measures set by the government and avoid unnecessary outings to risk bringing the virus back home with us. We have to work on our immune systems and prepare ourselves for countering any viruses and seasonal diseases such as common cold, flu, fever, and cough.

Most importantly, we have to gear up to offer our children—especially teenagers— the emotional support they need in a time of crisis like this and ensure that they don't become too anxious, worried or depressed about the pandemic.

In this guide, we shall talk about the methods and effective tools that parents can use to prevent anxiety in children and counter negativity. We shall look at ways of how to prevent depression from setting in when our kids practice social distancing from their friends and partners.

Chapter 1: Anxiety and Teen Depression during COVID-19

Social distancing, a requirement due to the pandemic, has been rather challenging for school-going folks. Not only are they missing out on a lot, but the lack of certainty about when things will be back to normal also adds to the mental stress and anxiety they experience. Children thrive on social interactions. Today's generation is mostly about connectivity and staying in touch with one another 24/7. Imagine taking that away from them? They are bound to act out, throw temper tantrums, exhibit frustration by picking fights over petty issues, and being distant and closed up emotionally.

Many children are mourning the loss of important milestones like their proms and graduations. Many had great opportunities to come up in terms of scholarships and internships at their favorite firms. All seems to have gone into a pending mode and the worst of it is no one can say for certain when all of this will come to an end. They are experiencing the social distancing blues and are finding this transition rather difficult and redefining.

The reason our children are facing the worst is that they are in the prime age of youth. This is supposedly the time when we create memories with friends that last a lifetime. It is the time when they fall in love for the first time, share some special moments with a beloved, have butterflies in their stomachs, support school teams during ball season and go through many things together.

This leaves parents rather confused as to how to make their time at home more fun, collaborative, and joyous. For if they don't, their children can easily go into depression or face quarantine fatigue. We are tasked with educating them, not just about the virus and its effects, but also about how they can keep their anxiety and stress managed. This will surely help them achieve a better state of mind and find some positivity in this otherwise gloomy situation.

How COVID-19 Is Affecting School-Going Kids

Researchers at the University of Bath, led by a clinical psychologist Maria Loades, explored how isolation and disease containment measures affected the mental health of both kids and teenagers. The study was published in the Journal of American Academy of Child and Adolescent Psychiatry. Following the current change of events, the researchers wanted to understand how abrupt changes in one's lifestyle and routine affected their mental health. Since many children and adolescents are suffering from loneliness caused by social distancing, it has led to many negative psychological effects such as post-traumatic distress (PTSD), confusion and anger, etc. In the review, Loades and her team of experts examined articles and studies from 1946 to 2020. Of the articles 83 met the inclusion criteria and 63 reported some form of isolation with a strong link to depression, anxiety, obsessive-compulsive disorder, trauma, and mental health concerns. The studies included approximately 51, 576 children with a mean age of 15.3 years. Of the studies articles, 43 were cross-sectional studies, 61 were observational, and 18 were longitudinal.

All the studies included some manipulation and biases, but longitudinal studies provided the most apt statistics and graphical measures. They were mostly based in Asian countries like China, Malaysia, Russia, Thailand, Iran, Korea, and India. They all implied that social distancing and loneliness increased the chances of developing depression over time. The majority of the participants in the studies self-reported feeling anxious and stressed out even five to nine years later. The duration of loneliness impacted how depressed or anxious the then adult was. It was also found that young adults were the most likely to feel the stress caused by prolonged isolation and loneliness. They were three times more likely to become depressed in the future due to social isolation. They reported seeking therapies and counseling to overcome anxiety and reduce the severity of the symptoms of depression.

If this remains the case, policymakers and public health officials will have to adhere to the rise in demand for therapists and social services for younger people because if this continues any longer, a generation of depressed and anxious people will be raised.

Another study also suggests that many children, as well as adults, will need clinical therapy to go back to living their normal lives as these many months are enough to form new habits and behaviors. Therefore, the normal we used to live in, won't seem normal at all and thus, many people will have a hard time adapting to the changes in the dynamics of how things work (Fegert et al., 2020).

Signs My Child Is Anxious

Teen anxiety and depression have been on the rise since the past decade. The advent of social media has led to bullying and encouraged teenagers to mock one another from behind screens. They are more exposed than ever to triggering marketing which compels them to believe in looking and feeling a certain way. When they don't, they feel less worthy. The National Institute of Mental Health estimates that an average of 32% of adolescents experience one or another form of anxiety, females more prone to it than males (Sorbring & Lansford, 2019). Now add to that picture the current crisis and you have depressed, anxious, and confused teenagers who don't know how to regulate their emotions and deal with the uncertainty of things. They feel powerless and out of control. Some are simply bored while others don't know what to make of their free time. Some are coping with grief and loss while others feel lonely and left out.

As a parent, you must be able to spot the symptoms of anxiety in your child before it becomes a disorder. Some of the most common and earliest signs of anxiety in children include:

- Feelings of worry, irrationality, and fear
- Extreme irritability
- Mood swings
- Sleep disruption
- Restlessness
- Tense muscles
- Poor focus and concentration
- Hyper-vigilance
- Heart palpitations etc.

By being exposed to multiple, rather confusing messages about COVID-19 from the media and news channels, they are bound to feel anxious. Teens that experience anxiety may gravitate towards harmful coping behaviors such as substance abuse or self-harming actions but it is important to teach them about why these don't offer long-term comfort and peace. They may be worried about their friends and families getting sick or dying. They may be scared that there hasn't been any promising news about when the virus will end or when a vaccine will be available to kill the virus from the roots.

Chapter 2: The 7 Essential Methods for Preventing Anxiety and Depression in Kids

Symptoms of anxiety may seep into teenagers as their feelings of isolation grow stronger. They have been bound at their homes and it can start to get boring. While they love spending time with you, they still miss being around their friends and video calls just don't cut it. There are always too many interruptions in the middle. Since they are no longer kids, they have also outgrown the phase where they enjoyed playing games with you. Besides, how many game nights can one have in a week? Even though Netflix, Amazon Prime, and Disney+ have taken up some of their free time, even streaming becomes boring after a few days when one can't decide which show is appropriate to watch with the whole family. You can sense their annoyance becoming more visible. But the situation isn't as grim as you think it is.

There is so much you can do to ease their tension and stress. There are tons of things you can do to spend quality time together with your teenager. Look at this time as a blessing in disguise rather than a burden. True, conflicts have increased and everyone seems to have a mood of their own but aim to make the most of this time to find things to connect and bond. Soon, your children will be headed for college or moving out and you will go back to thinking about the time you had with them and how beautiful it was.

Since you want them to be happy and comfortable instead of annoyed, bored, or frustrated, the first thing you need to do is alleviate their stress and anxiety. Even an ounce of stress in them can turn wonderful times stressful. No matter what you do, they won't feel the joy if they are anxious about their future and all that it holds.

Thus, to help parents get started on the right foot and connect with their adolescents better and eliminate all signs of anxiety and depression from them, we are going to recommend seven effective methods aka parenting tips to help them cope with their anxiety in a much more healthy, and capable way. Let's briefly review what they are here before going into the depth of each.

Stay Posted

Staying posted or updated about what's going on in the world through reliable and official channels is the first step to overcoming anxiety. A lot of times, misinformation can trigger anxiety. Wrong statistics, false news, manipulated information, and statistics can easily add to one's anxiety. Thus, help them find resources that offer confirmed and verified news. Tell them strictly not to believe in everything they hear or read about and teach them how to check for the reliability of the information first before sharing it with others.

Show Empathy

Showing empathy means letting them know that you acknowledge what they are going through. Having a strong support system in their lives is what they need the most, especially during the pandemic. They are worried about their friends, education, and dreams. They need someone to hear them out and let them know that things will be alright. Do we not feel a whole lot better when we know we have a strong support system? Let children feel the same support and validation.

Practice Mindfulness

A clear head, free from negative thoughts and feelings, is a space for creativity and positivity. Encourage your teens to practice mindfulness and become more aware of their surroundings and the present. Show them how they can pay gratitude for the blessings they have, even in such negative and scary times. Teach them to regulate their emotions better by using techniques like deep breathing to induce happiness and calmness in their bodies.

Provide Structure and Routines

Following the same structure and routine as before can also prevent anxiety and depression. If they wake up at the same time every day as they did for their school and then followed the same routine, they will have less free time to think about all that is going on around the world. Routines and structure provide predictability—the one thing your child needs the most right now. Having structure also helps kids to know what is expected of them.

Teach Coping Skills

Coping skills build resilience in children. They learn to move from things in healthy ways. It prevents them from gravitating towards negative behaviors and self-harming actions. Keeping the current state in mind, they are more anxious than ever. They are missing their friends and have too much free time on their hands. An empty mind is like a house for the devil. It is easier to allow negativity to set the house in the mind and become depressed. However, if children know how to overcome their grief, feelings of loneliness, and frustration, they are in a much better state to regulate their emotions and improve their behaviors.

Find Ways to Stay Connected

The teenage years are the time to develop new bonds, and connections. COVID-19 has taken that away from them. They can't meet their friends, hang out with them, go to the movies with them, or play games outside. They are struggling with the intense need to connect with their peers and miss school. But just because they can't physically meet their friends doesn't mean they can't meet them virtually. Also, if they promise to maintain social distancing, they can go on a walk with them or ride a bike with them too— of course, while practicing the safety measures. The reason staying connected is urged upon so much is because it keeps your child engaged and occupied. They shouldn't distance themselves emotionally from their friends as it may trigger anxiety, depression, and sadness.

Stay Active

Staying active allows children to take care of their bodies' physical as well as emotional needs. It prevents weight gain and worry caused by stress. It promises a stronger immune system and healthy stamina. According to WHO, we must all try to boost our immunity by eating the right foods, exercising, and sleeping for a good eight hours every night. Exercise is food for the body. When we sweat, we improve blood circulation. When we get those hands and feet moving, we improve our flexibility. When we meditate, we allow our mind to release all negative thoughts. Doesn't that sound like a good state to be in? Thus, encourage the same in your children too.

Chapter 3: Essential Parenting Skill #1—Stay Posted

The World Health Organization lists COVID-19 related infodemic as dangerous as the pandemic itself. Information containing preventive measures that don't come verified, turning to Ayurveda or herbal cures to treat COVID-19 instead of recommended drugs and medications from medical experts, or not following the guidelines on how to maintain distance, wash hands, or cover your mouth with a mask because an article suggests so, can be destructive.

Not to mention, there are as many as a hundred different conspiracy theories put forward by people with no knowledge about what they are or their impact on the masses have also come to light. Some still believe that the virus is the government's intervention to control the population and gather information about them (Shih, 2020), China's revenge on us to ruin our economy (Beusekom, 2020), or personal interests such as that of the business magnate to insert a tracking chip into all of us via a vaccine to track our movements and manipulate our actions and behaviors (Goodman & Carmichael, 2020).

Such theories have done nothing but promote new types of xenophobia where people blame a certain country or race to have been responsible for the outbreak. China, which was hit worst during the start of 2020, has received the most hate followed by other East Asian countries for their inability to control the spread of the virus or for not warning the world about it earlier.

When memes, pictures, and videos promoting xenophobia are uploaded, liked, and shared, people fail to realize the severity of the situation we are currently in and start to mock the virus or the need to seek protection and go into isolation. Even today, there are hundreds and thousands of people who are against the use of masks to protect themselves and potentially others from becoming exposed to the virus because they don't think that the virus will get to them or that they are strong enough to fight it off. What they fail to realize is that it is no longer about them contracting the virus but rather about other people and demographics. For instance, from day 1, we were aware that people above the age of 50 are most vulnerable to the virus due to a weaker immune system, but there is very little that we have done to control its spread.

When we are exposed to fake or misleading information daily, it can also fuel confusion and a state of panic. I hope there isn't a need to remind people how stores were out of toilet paper in a matter of minutes after being restocked. The less informed we are, the more dangerous it is. But what is even more dangerous than that is being exposed to wrong information.

Thus the first parenting goal or skill is to limit the amount of misleading confusing information your child is exposed to. We need to keep a check on what they are watching online and what they are believing blindly.

Fake News and its Impact

According to a pilot study, believing fake news is bad for your heart and induces stress (Barlow, 2018). The study was led by a team of researchers at Manchester Metropolitan University. The researchers believe that people with low "information discernment (ID)" don't question the viability of the news or how reliable the source is. This causes them to exhibit unhealthy symptoms of mental stress.

The study consisted of 18, twenty-four-years-old males. They were asked questions about how they consumed information and news. The questions included topics like what were their favorite sites to view news, did they always turn to them for the latest updates, did they try to double-check the information they were consuming by going to another news portal, did they check for its reliability before sharing it with others online, and whether or not they opened the attached links and studies to see the facts for themselves. After the participants had answered the questions, they were connected to a Finometer—a device that measures cardiovascular reactivity. The device also measured their heartbeat, arterial blood flow, and tracked their eye movement. After they were connected to the Finometer, they were presented with six news stories to read based on a religious theme.

This was done to understand the difference between high and low information discerners. Did they read the whole story before believing a thing or did they just scroll through it mindlessly? As per the findings, the low ID group only concentrated on the first few paragraphs of the story whereas the high ID group scanned the whole news by giving special attention to the graphical information too.

Following that, the participants were asked to attempt an impossible-to-complete word search. This was to make them feel a little stressed. They were made to believe that by doing so, they were helping another participant win £100. The received information falsely revealed that the participant for whom they were trying to win had strong religious beliefs. Participants were asked about how they felt about the task and their physiological responses were captured.

The findings revealed that when participants that had low ID received false information about the other participants, their emotional and cardiovascular response was poor as compared to those with a high ID who seemed to have healthier responses.

Researchers also found that when participants with low ID were presented with false information in a stressful situation, they had a flawed 'threat' response. Their bodies produced more of the stress hormone cortisol which brought about unhelpful cardiac responses as well as caused erratic reading behavior. This type of stress, as per the researchers, can lead to psychological problems too and it was also evident in the research study. The participants with low ID lacked self-confidence and had a poor sense of self-worth. They were unable to make balanced, well-informed judgments, which is essential for our well-being. Principal investigator of the pilot study, Dr. Geoff Walton believes that people who are unable to make good judgments about the information they come across online, on TV or in the newspaper, experience a negative physical response, which indicates that fake or false news is bad for your health.

On the contrary, those that are good at making judgments about the information they come across on said channels of communication tend to have a more positive and healthier physical response to it. Given the amount of misleading and fake news we and our children are exposed to daily, it poses a rather concerning and worrying threat to our physical and mental health.

Infodemic—Get Your Facts Straight

One of the most important things at this date and time is to get your facts straight. Misleading information, as we now know, can increase anxiety and cause depression. Therefore, to promote health and wellness and prevent the onset of anxiety in children, it is best to stay true to the facts and only rely on authentic information coming straight from reliable resources, because believe it or not, the infodemic is a greater pandemic than COVID-19 itself today.

Here are some ways parents can save teenagers from giving into false and fake news and become more upset than they already are.

Turn To Authentic/Official Sources for Updates

The best way to counter misleading or fake news is to only turn to official portals for all COVID-19 related news. They may report things late or take time to update their website but only because they are bound to post things that have been verified from multiple sources. There is no room for errors or doubtful information on sites like the World Health Organization or Centre for Disease Control, or National Health Service if you are in the UK. Also, sites ending with ".gov", or ".edu" are the most reliable among others as they indicate that they are either government-owned websites or by academic institutions aimed at research and studies.

Don't Turn a Blind Eye

Everyone we talk or turn to seems to have figured it all out. They will tell you of herbal remedies, alternative medications, and therapies to 'cure'

COVID-19. But do you think that the things random people come up with can be trusted over the word of the officials, scientists, and medical experts who still aren't 100% sure about the basics of the virus, its extent, its mutation or how it's transmitted in communities? The point being, don't believe everything you hear or see. Be vigilant and rely only on news coming directly from the official channels and medical experts. They know more about the virus than anyone else. Let them be the only guide you trust and stay away from conspiracy theories like it was all planned and concocted in a lab somewhere in Wuhan, China. The only thing you need to worry about is how you are going to protect yourself and your family from the virus and play a key role in helping stop its spread.

Check Reliability

Many people circulate messages without checking for its reliability. How can you be certain that the information you are about to share or have just received is coming from the official channels and is verified news? Whenever you receive something shady or remotely worrisome, always check for its source and authenticity. Is the article coming from a professional expert? Is the article dated recently? Are the links provided active and real? Are the numbers on the studies real or manipulated to increase impact and share-ability?

Admit that Things Can Be Manipulated

It happens and it happens a lot. There is an exaggeration of numbers, untrue facts stated as true, and broken links attached. There are also misleading headlines or ones that are click baits. It is best to avoid clicking on them or looking up to them for reliable information.

Unplug

Sometimes, excess of anything becomes harmful too. The majority of the information about the pandemic is indeed available online, sometimes, too much of it can lead to anxiety. Isolation periods and lockdowns get longer within a day's notice which can lead to further anxiety. Moreover, the kids can get exposed to misleading or confusing information, which is why it may be in their best interest, and yours too, to unplug from time to time. Look for other activities and passions to spend your free time on. Bond together, have meaningful conversations, start a new project together, etc. The more engaged you remain, the less time you will have to tune into social media, and less will be the exposure.

Check Their Biases

We can be too quick to judge and move on. It is human tendency to quickly believe things they already support or know of and disregard information they don't like or support. For example, if you don't support a political figure, there are fewer chances that you will listen to anything they say or believe in it. Teenagers too, have a hard time being open to information they don't agree with. However, at a time like this, we have to adapt better. Our goal shouldn't be to focus on who is saying what but on rather what they are saying. If it makes sense and seems a rational, calculated, and reliable piece of information, it is best to keep your biases aside.

Chapter 4: Essential Parenting Skill #2—Show Empathy

Living in seclusion for no one knows how long can lead to quarantine fatigue, a term used to describe exhaustion caused by the new restrictive lifestyle that we are forced to adapt to. In many cases, your teen might feel like hitting a wall, says Noelle Wittliff, a South Pasadena-based licensed marriage and family therapist. Having worked with families and teenagers, she understands the emotional turmoil children are going through thanks to the pandemic. She believes that children are craving to leave the house, go out, hang out with their friends, and connect with them like old times. The online connection, although it seems promising, just doesn't cut it.

Generally, this particular phase we call adolescence is marked by feelings of invincibility and impulsivity. If we recall the time when we were young and energetic and then try to make note of what our children are missing out on, we understand the reasons for their anxiety and depression. This is the time when children begin to separate from their parents and make friends out of choice. They seek companionship elsewhere and work on stabilizing bonds with their partners and peers. Since they have been confined to their homes with their parents, their need for social interaction and independence has been crushed.

They are sad because the prom has been canceled. They are sad that they won't make it to their graduation, they are sad because they miss their friends and teachers. The schools shut down so abruptly that many friends even didn't get a chance to say a proper farewell.

As a parent, the second most important thing you need right now is to show empathy. You need to tell them that you understand what they are going through and are sad that they have to face such uncertainty. Showing empathy involves not just consoling or trying to see things from their perspective but also listening and communicating in a way that they feel heard and validated.

Why Show Empathy?

For starters, showing empathy towards others is one of the greatest gifts to give others. It is an art that requires attention, care, and a strong need to strengthen the connection with the speaker. It takes guts to be able to put yourself in someone else's shoes. It takes guts to understand another person's point of view.

For you, it is a chance to get to know your teen better by building a bridge of communication. When you decide to show empathy, you tell them that your emotional needs will be taken care of. You tell them that you will support them every step of the way and help them cope with the new normal in healthy ways.

You are not only paving way for openness but also trying to become a friend with your child when you try to show empathy.

Another reason showing empathy is important is because sooner or later, your kids are going to move on and get busy in their own lives. They will be expected to form new bonds, meet new people, and have a job and a family. They need to know how to be supportive as well as express themselves better. They need not see the world from their eyes alone but also from others. When they see you showing empathy and notice how reassuring it feels, they are likely to take it on too. Empathy is one of the many essential social skills they need to develop as it will help them maintain healthy relationships in adulthood.

Secondly, empathy also builds resilience in children. When they feel appreciated, validated, and cared for, when they feel that their feelings and thoughts matter to someone, when they feel that their opinions hold value, it helps them build resilience. They feel gratitude for the things that they have instead of feeling sorry or getting stuck over one thing. Resilience is the ability to move on from failure or loss and learn to cope.

Finally, your teenager has lost most of their privileges and independence after the recent turn of events. They can't drive around, go to a gym or for a jog in the park, they can't meet their friends and go watch a movie. They are frustrated because they have to stay indoors and away from all the things they loved doing. Living indoors has also bound them to many household chores and they are back at being supervised 24/7 by their parents and siblings. This often makes them act out due to boredom and anger. Being understood, and heard can make a huge difference in toning down the level of frustration that's brewing inside them.

How to Be Empathetic Towards Children during these Tough Times

To get started with being empathetic is to know that whatever your child is going through is pretty normal as long as they don't depict any signs of extreme stress and anxiety. Showing empathy doesn't mean that you forget all the rules and structure you laid in practice. It simply means giving them the chance to feel a little better about their situation by helping them unburden and not let that frustration build up. It is about raising their self-esteem and self-worth by acknowledging their loss and sadness. There are multiple ways to do so and some have been highlighted below.

Connect with Others

In times like these, we often become focused on ourselves and forget about others and what they are going through. You may, unintentionally, be ignoring your children or assuming that they are alright but you need to reach out and keep a check on them. You have to find ways to connect with them and also with others in your community so that they do the same. To fight feelings of isolation, having someone's sincere company and presence can mean the world. Being a part of your child's life and engaging in helpful actions like donating things to charities, or supporting a social cause can increase their feelings of connectedness. Of course, you have to maintain social distancing but that shouldn't stop you from offering your moral support to others. The best time to get in touch with people you rarely talked to in the past, is now.

Be Compassionate

It is okay if there are days when your kids spend all the time in front of a TV or in their rooms with a locked door. Like you, they are also trying to make the best of the situation. Some days, you may feel like nagging or being harsh with them, but try not to. Instead, reach out to them with compassion. For all that we know, you two are stuck in this for longer than anticipated, so there is no point in trying to fight with your child over petty issues. Maybe the reason for the change in their behavior is because they are finding it hard to cope with the situation. Or perhaps they are too anxious and don't know how to manage the barricade of feelings. Show compassion. Don't try to be nagging all the time and let them have their space.

Stay Aware of Their Needs

Remember the time when you were a child or a budding adult, what were the things you needed the most? Now focus on how the pandemic has affected the life of your child. Try to visualize the things they are missing out on and how it might make them feel. They may need more than just your emotional support. Try to fill the voids by doing things together. Take up a project and work on it together. Show appreciation for the help they offer around the house. Help them with their homework.

Chapter 5: Vital Parenting Skill #3—Stick to Routine and Provide Structure

As kids are confined to homes, there will be times when they will test your limits. They would want to go out, hang out with their friends. Since this isn't a possibility, they will try to manipulate you into other ways where they start to demand things from you simply because they are bored or don't know what to do in the ample amount of time they have. The first few weeks after the lockdown have passed and the things that interested them, in the beginning, don't anymore. They have watched all the interesting shows on Netflix, watched their favorite movies over and over again, and are done checking their phones every five minutes. What they need aren't more activities but rather a structure and routine.

Not long ago, they always seemed busy. They had school assignments to work on, limited TV time, short breaks for dinner. They never had any free time. How about restarting with the same routine again? Structure and routines allow them to follow the clock. They wake up at a certain time, go to bed at a fixed time, spend time working on their assignments at a certain time, etc. When bound by a consistent routine, they are less likely to act out or resort to negative behaviors like needless disagreements, secrecy, and deceit.

Routines, when put into practice, give them a list of all the things they are expected to do throughout the day.

Why Kids Need Structure

During a time as such creating a routine helps children, teenagers in particular, in several ways. Since they are the toughest to deal with, thanks to their moodiness and rebellious nature, having a routine provides them with some predictability and structure. They desperately need that as uncertainty about their future has them all worked up. A routine promotes reassurance. It promotes a sense of safety. It also gives the mind something to focus on and less time to think negatively.

Most teenagers are also impulsive by nature. They will act out harshly when they feel annoyed or frustrated. Structure not only keeps them engaged, but it also limits misbehavior. It gives them clear directions of what is expected of them and how they must do it. Take household chores for instance. If they have vague instructions about how to do them, they are going to be least motivated about them. This will lead to poor performance and guaranteed failure which will cause more frustration. They will most probably argue with the one who set the chore for them or act out.

Thirdly, the structure provides organization. Everything expected of them is consistent and planned out in advance. This leaves fewer chances of mistakes. Routines also prevent procrastination and improve efficiency. Everything gets done promptly and with effectiveness. The more elaborative the rules, the less anxiety your child will experience.

Establishing Routines for Teenagers

Now that we know of the importance of routine and how they promote wellness and mental health in children, below are some great ways to get started with routines. But before we do that, here's a helpful tip: Whenever deciding on a routine or structure, let your child have a say in it. It will make them feel like an important part of the rules and they will be more willing to adhere to them. Sit together and seek their input on how you can work out a plan that works best for you both. This will minimize acting out, temper tantrums, and arguments in the future.

Set Clear Expectations

Start with setting realistic and clear expectations. They should, at all times, know what is expected of them. Having clear goals and expectations increases the likelihood of their accomplishment. When children are unable to decipher what is expected of them, they feel confused and aren't able to give 100% to anything. Thus, if you want them to follow a routine or structure, let them know the rules first.

Have Bedtime and Wake Up Routines

Since no one is going to school or the office anymore, it may seem tempting to sleep in till late. If your children's school isn't offering online classes and they are free for the whole semester, don't encourage the habit of sleeping in till late in the morning. Start the day early and go through the routines as if it were a regular school day. Don't allow them to stay in their jammies all day because then, it will become a habit. The same goes for bedtime routines. It is understandable to stretch the bedtime to an hour or two but not more than that, especially on weeknights. Having a routine will allow their physiological system to maintain a balance between rest periods and activity. It won't confuse the mind about when to go to sleep and when to wake up. It can also promote the onset of fatigue during odd hours of the day which can lead to hormonal imbalances.

Schedule Meal Times

The same applies to meal times. If they used to have their first meal of the day around 7:00 am, let that remain a staple. They may act annoyed but be strict about it. Eating at inappropriate times upsets the digestive system. Additionally, when food is offered at regular timings, there are fewer instances of feeling hungry. While at it, if you notice them eating at odd hours or feeling hungry all the time, teach them to differentiate between different types of hunger. Are they eating simply because they are bored or are they eating to feel less lonely?

Allow Breaks in Between

Realistically speaking, they are on a break currently. They deserve some time to cool off. They don't need to be disciplined all the time. Allow some free time during the day at regular intervals to uplift their mood and engage in things they are passionate about. It can mean playing their favorite video games, for some, it may be watching TV or listening to music. Having breaks in between will give their mind some rest and recharging time. Fun-breaks can also alleviate stress and anxiety.

Encourage Creative Outlets

Encourage them to pursue their hobbies and interests now that they have some free time on their hands. However, be sure to allow a certain time of the day to engage in them. Hobbies foster creativity and give children something to enjoy.

Chapter 6: Essential Parenting Skill #4—Practice Mindfulness

Teenagers are worried more than ever about their future and what it will look like. Their studies have come to an abrupt halt, they don't know what expectations companies will have from them and whether they will ever find a job of their choosing in such economically harsh times or not. Will they be able to get any summer jobs if the country continues to stay in a lockdown or be able to keep the one they have in case the stores don't reopen? These are genuine concerns that can keep them awake at night and cause severe anxiety.

But this worry is understandable. Nearly every generation ever since the existence of humanity, has gone through some economic recession period. It isn't the first time that people are being laid off. Some wars destabilized the entire continents, there were pandemics and the global recession that made our elders lose their job and sit at home. You can always encourage your children to read about it and learn how they coped with the ever-changing world and raised their value. Secondly, to reduce their anxiety, try using mindfulness techniques.

Being mindful requires a sane and present mind. When practicing mindfulness, one needs to focus on the present and stop worrying about the past or the future. When you can acknowledge and take in all that is happening around you, your mind becomes relaxed and calm. It is easy to focus on the things that aren't in our control, such as the pandemic, but it is more fruitful and peaceful to focus on the things that are in our control and be grateful for the blessings. When we feel focused, we are better able to steer in the right direction with rational thinking and manage our emotions.

Presently, most of the time our kids spent during commutes, at school and going out with friends isn't available. They have more free time today than they ever had before. The lack of activities and routines can lead the mind into thinking negatively. As parents, we need to make the most of that time, and practicing mindfulness seems like a good and beneficial option.

Being mindful takes time but once your children get the hang of it, they will begin to enjoy it. Their thoughts will become positive and intentional. They won't worry about what to do with their free time but rather, would already have many ideas to work upon as mindfulness boosts creativity and focus.

How Mindfulness Can Help Teenagers

Although life is complicated for teenagers generally, it won't be easy unless they do something about it. Remember the time when they were young and feared entering high school? Their concerns and excitement kept their mind occupied at all times. It seemed like a challenge back then. But now that they have made it and are in the second, third, fourth year, it doesn't seem as tough. This means that we are naturally capable of adjusting to a new normal. Right now they are worried about their future but two to three years down the line and they will be laughing about this among their college friends. But this isn't easy for everyone. For some, transitions are the hardest to make. This is where social skills come into play. This is the part where they need to learn some excellent and healthy coping skills to regulate their emotions better. But it all starts with a relaxed and eager mind which mindfulness can help achieve.

Some of the many benefits of mindfulness are:

- Reduced anxiety. When children can switch from thinking negative to positive, their anxiety levels are reduced too.
- Better quality of sleep. To get a good night's sleep, you need a clear and relaxed mind. Mindfulness techniques help students achieve just that!
- Improved emotional regulation. Children, and especially teenagers, can be highly emotional. The many bodily and hormonal transitions they are going through are enough to cause stress and anxiety. They were worried about how they look, if they will be socially acceptable or not, and whether somebody will like them or not. Introducing them to mindfulness and how it works can help them cope with negative emotions

better. They can connect with their inner self better and not let it bully them into thinking that they aren't good enough.

- A focused mind. When children practice mindful techniques regularly, they improve their attention span too. They can focus on one thing for a longer period than before.

How to Practice Mindfulness—A Guide for Teenagers

Being mindful involves slowing down and focusing on the things in the present. It sounds simple but when one is stressed out or anxious, it can become rather challenging. But since the goal is to get started, no matter how big or small the effort, here are a few strategies to improve your focus and feel good about the present despite the current circumstances.

Stop Multitasking

There was a time not long ago when professionals urged us to multitask. They believed it helped finish tasks faster. But they failed to acknowledge one important thing—it butchers the quality of it. When we attempt to multi-task, we are unable to focus on a single task completed. Our brain isn't designed to do so. It is designed to single-task.

With so much time spent at home, teens are expected to help with the chores. But they don't want to put their phones down even for a minute either. Doing both can lead to more stress and anxiety as the brain becomes confused about the order of things, the specific demands of each, and becomes stressed. Thus, if you want to get all the chores done correctly and promptly, ask them to focus on just one thing at a time.

Use the STOP Strategy

The acronym STOP stands for the following

S - Stop whatever you are doing and take a moment to breathe

T - Take a deep breath and be aware of the action

O - Observe the many sensations, thoughts, and emotions you go through

P - Pause and be still for a few minutes to soak in positive energy from your surroundings before going about your day.

This is, by far, the easiest and most effective way to practice deep breathing and become more aware of the thoughts in your mind, and the sensations in your body.

Go for a Walk

Sounds rather conflicting to what we are told by public health officials, going for a walk in the park or the neighborhood is only dangerous if social distancing protocols aren't being followed. Going outside and breathing into the fresh air, hearing the chirping of the birds, watching the tree's branches sway with the wind, and the sun shining on your face can help you feel better and improve the functioning of your senses. The calmer you feel, the lesser the chatter in your mind.

Make Peace with Ambiguity

The virus isn't going anywhere anytime soon. Even if a vaccine is developed, it will take months of testing both on animals and later on humans to see if the drug is beneficial in the long run or not. After that, it will take months before everyone can afford one. That being said, you can't waste your time thinking about the things that aren't in your control. No one can say what will happen for certain in the future and what it will look like. Thus, there is no point in trying to get all worked up because of it. Your teenager shouldn't let this fear of the uncertainty get to them. If they can't change their current state, there is no point worrying about it. Instead, motivate them to acknowledge the uncertainty and make peace with it.

Show Gratitude

Amid the craziness, it can be hard to focus on the brighter side of things, but as their parent, you have to motivate them to. Focusing on the positive will keep their mind away from the negativity and the disappointment they face. Ask them to come up with three to five things they are grateful for in their lives every day. These can be as simple as good food on the table, good health, a roof over their heads, their family members and their safety, and friends they can count on. Acknowledgment of these will allow them to stay positive and not fall into depression or suffer from anxiety.

Chapter 7: Vital Parenting Skill #5–Find Ways to Stay Connected

The need for practical distancing has put a pause on normal social activities like backyard barbecues, movie nights, date nights, sleepovers with friends, musical concerts and festivals, school functions and sports events, etc. While it is imperative that you maintain distance from others to flatten the curve, it doesn't mean cutting out on your friends and relatives in the literal sense. Social interactions must still be made, only virtually. Staying connected has become more important than ever as it promotes well-being and mental health when you have someone to talk to.

Social connections bring us closer to one another and make us feel an integral part of the community. Man has always been a social animal. His need for social interactions, to communicate, to express love and complain can't be denied. Every person we come across daily or on a routine basis plays some part in our lives–even the bus driver that comes to pick our children up every day or the garbage truck driver or the mailman. Each leaves behind some impression on our mind and mental health.

During these scary and uncertain times, we are all experiencing one or more forms of physical or cognitive symptoms of loneliness. We are confined in our homes with not much to do other than just eat, sleep, and watch TV. We desperately want to go out, hang out with our co-workers, friends, and relatives. News flash: teenagers feel the same.

They are bored and miss their friends. They are in that phase of their lives where they value their friends more than their siblings and parents because they can connect better with them. But since everything has been shut down, they feel stressed which is a scientifically proven aftermath of social isolation. The need for the physical touch even if it just means shaking hands, hugging each other, or patting each other's back is an ultimate stress-reducer. Teenagers, upon meeting one another during school hours mostly stayed in some form of physical touch. Physical touch floods our body with the bonding hormone, medically referred to as oxytocin. It is known to improve immune response and mental health. Since it is impossible to feel that way during the current pandemic, we have to let our children stay connected in some other ways.

How Does Social Connectedness Impact Our Health?

During these unique circumstances, you can't completely disconnect with everyone. We all have to come together virtually to support each other and look after each other.

Why?

Being isolated prevents us from expressing our feelings about both complaints and affection. It prevents us from venting out and thus, leads to unwanted stress. Children who are not encouraged to speak their minds have poor self-confidence and self-worth. They feel unvalued and unloved by their parents and others. When someone gifts us their attention and affection, it automatically reduces the stress hormones. When the body feels less stressed, the immune system is strengthened. Ongoing research also promises many other health benefits of staying connected. These include longer life, happier outlook towards life, improved cognitive skills and memory, and increased motivation to look after one's self.

Some studies stress the importance of friendships and their link with providing emotional support and intellectual stimulation in difficult times. With social distancing protocols in place, stress can easily find a way to creep up on us and leave us feeling depressed and annoyed.

How to Stay Socially Connected with Peers

Thanks to the internet, there are now tons of ways to stay in touch with friends and family virtually. Apps like Zoom, Hangouts, WhatsApp, and Facebook have made it easier to stay in touch with our loved ones and communicate with them whenever needed. Since this current generation is the master of apps and social media platforms, they haven't given up on their friends. They are constantly in touch with them virtually. As discussed above, staying connected is imperative. Here are some ways to further encourage social interactions without actually leaving the house.

Catch-up Virtually

Encourage teenagers to schedule video calls via several social networks to keep a check on one another. Being in touch allows them to feel connected as they are all going through the same challenges. This also goes for adults. They too should set up virtual hangouts with distant relatives, especially older ones to ensure their health is in prime condition and they aren't feeling left out.

Play Games

In their free time, your children can schedule games to be played together. There are thousands of free apps that allow participants to connect and play against one another or as a team. You can play Uno, Monopoly, chess, Scrabble, word puzzles, and similar board games that require more than one player. You can also play games as a family by organizing a game night.

Host Movie Nights

Thanks to Netflix Party, integration into the famous online entertainment service, it allows children to sync video playback with their friends. Every individual who is a part of the party can pause, play, rewind, or fast forward the movie from their screens so that everyone in the group views it at the same time. There is also a chat room they can use to share their thoughts about the movie or the show or simply talk with one another. The best thing about it is that only those in the group can send an invite which eliminates the chance of any stranger joining the chat room.

Write a Letter

This one is an old-school trick. Before WhatsApp or even text messaging, people used to write one another heartfelt letters to express their feelings and compassion. You can encourage your child to do the same and mail it to their pals. If writing a letter is too much, they can write an email instead and talk to their friends. The joy of finding that one email from a loved one is incomparable to a text that is received within seconds. The time they spend waiting for it to arrive is both pleasant and torturous.

Start an Activity Together

Although young boys may not be interested in this as much, teen girls can do stuff virtually-together. For example, they can all start a book club and read the same book throughout the week. They can later discuss the prose, characters, and story. If they are into fashion, they can sew masks or scarves for poor people and donate them to the homeless. They can also bake cookies for everyone in the neighborhood to spread some joy in these tough times.

Chapter 8: Essential Parenting Skill #6–Teach Coping Skills

When children are worried, stressed out, or anxious, it makes thinking rationally harder. They may fail to understand how to deal with the stress and resort to negative behaviors to feel better. The most common signs that your child is stressed or anxious include excessive clinginess, aggressiveness, emotional meltdowns, tearfulness, and regression among other behaviors. Some kids may often report headaches, dizziness, a racing heart, stomachaches, and poor sleep patterns.

As a parent, it is your job to take care of both their emotional and physical complaints. You have to teach them healthy and positive ways to express themselves as well as manage their anxiety. They need to address their feelings with a positive attitude and not give in to the overwhelming feelings. They need to know how to cope after a setback and move forward in their lives without clinging to the past. Easier said than done, it isn't easy for parents to connect with their children as they have grown into teenagers. They are rebellious and can counter your words and actions with even smarter comebacks. They may not understand why you need to sort things for them when they can do it themselves. But they can't and it's visible in the ways they are acting around the house. The first thing you need to do to connect with them is to offer them a safe space to be themselves. This means that they shouldn't feel the need to keep things bottled up inside and feel no shame in expressing their emotions. They need to know that expressing emotions doesn't make them weak.

Why Kids Need to Learn to Manage Stress and Anxiety

Stress is an uncomfortable feeling. But it is also a reality of life. Some stress is known healthy as it keeps us driven and motivated to change our current state. However, for kids who don't know how to manage anxiety, it can be detrimental to their health. It makes them uncomfortable and they do what they can to escape that. This escaping from a state of discomfort to comfort is what we call coping. How we cope with the various challenges we face in life is what determines whether we are stronger or weak.

The reason kids need to learn to manage stress is that it can make life difficult for them. They may report sleeplessness, depression, irritability, and anger. When we are stressed, our body releases cortisol which our immune system has to fight against. Now, had the situation been any different, we would have suggested that we let our immune system work things out. But we need it to fight against the more dangerous and potentially life-threatening virus. We can't have it doing overtime and making the body and all its organs face the consequences. Over time, stress can also lead to serious health issues such as high blood pressure, cardiovascular problems, and anxiety disorders. Thus, we need to eliminate the causes or prepare our children to fight against it.

In general, there are two approaches to counter bad feelings both, positive and negative. Negative coping strategies may seem tempting and offer short-term relief but they don't address the problem at the core. Meaning, you are soon going to find yourself in the same dark pit as before. If you get addicted, it can be harmful in the long run too. Thus, you don't want your kids to rely on quick fixes to overcome their anxiety and stress. Positive coping strategies, on the other hand, enhance emotional health, promote well-being, and build confidence in a child's strengths. They also help strengthen relationships and make kids more resilient. They may require more time to work and need more willingness and investment but the benefits are long-term and prosperous. Positive and healthy ways of coping are also preventive strategies as they not only offer relief from the existing anxiety but also reduces the chances of experiencing it later.

Our goal, as parents, should be to expose our kids to positive coping strategies.

Stress Management Strategies for Kids

Your role is a crucial one in developing healthy coping skills among children. Some of the most effective ways to get started are mentioned below.

Encourage Deep Breathing Exercises

Deep breathing helps relax our mind and body. It is the most innovative and effective way to tone down a panic attack and calm an anxious person. The best thing about this is how simple it is. Let your child experience calmness by taking a deep breath, holding it in, and then releasing it. Deep breathing activates our parasympathetic nervous system. In simpler terms, it reduces the feelings of fear and distress and allows the breather to feel a sense of calm. Teaching kids about using this strategy as the means to start their day can uplift their mood and make their minds more relaxed and creative. With COVID-19 ruining all their plans for the year, they can use this to alleviate their stress and manage their anxiety.

Give Their Feelings a Name

Before they start with the deep breathing technique, let them analyze the reasons for their stress and anxiety. They need to know what they are feeling exactly first. Many children are unable to distinguish between fear and anxiety or anger and frustration. Some think they are synonymous but as adults, we know that they aren't. Therefore, before aiming to control their emotional beast, they need to label the feelings they are going through.

Stop Worrying about Things They Can't Control

There is not much that you can control during the pandemic. Even if you are taking all the precautionary measures recommended by the public health officers, you can't be certain that everyone else is following them too. This means that as long as everyone doesn't abide by the rules and follow the instructions, our condition wouldn't change. This can lead to anger and frustration among teenagers who are waiting for the day to feel freedom again. Showing empathy and teaching them coping skills to combat situations out of their control is another important aspect. You need to shift their focus from the things they can't control to the ones they can and stop worrying about the former. Remind them that although they can't control or manipulate everyone's freedom of speech, they are accountable for their actions, words, and behaviors.

Offer Compassion and Validation

Children of all ages want to be heard. They want their concerns listened to with a compassionate and supportive heart. They want to feel validated and appreciated. They also need their parents to show empathy and validate their fears by acknowledging them. Let your kid know that they are not alone in this. Let them see that they have your moral, physical, and emotional support through thick and thin.

Empower Them

Ask for their input in things. Show them how they can help. Engage them in projects of their interest so that they don't feel left out. When we allow children to act like adults and empower them with some responsibility, they feel valued. Reassure them that their health is in their hands. Tell them that they need to protect themselves by practicing proper handwashing, wearing gloves when going out for a run, and wearing a mask. Teach them about the cough and sneezing etiquette and give them the responsibility to ensure that their presence doesn't become an inconvenience to anyone. They will be more willing to stick with the rules when they feel in control.

Chapter 9: Essential Parenting Skill #7–Stay Active

As adults, we are fully aware of the many health benefits of staying active. As we cope with the new normal, every aspect of our lives has turned upside down. Businesses have closed down, social distancing measures have been put in place, homes have turned into office cubicles, classes are conducted online; we don't know what is next. With every business temporarily on hold, gyms and fitness centers are no exception. Try to recall the times when we would gladly skip leg day or purposely busy ourselves into work to avoid going to the gym. Well, look at us now—desperate to get out of the house, even if it means going to the gym. The good news, however, is that we are coming to this realization that we don't need gyms to stay healthy and in shape. We simply need a workout plan that keeps us in shape and gets rid of the excess fat.

But many of us are skipping workouts out of choice when this is the time we need to work out the most. According to public health officials, we have to work out to boost our immunity, build stamina, and give our muscles the flexibility they need to stay in shape. Too much muscle relaxation abruptly, especially for someone who worked out religiously can lead to poor muscle flexibility over time and make life rather painful.

Another important reason why we need to stay active and push our children to do the same is that when our bodies are constantly in stress or survival mode, it can trigger the fight or flight response. When the body of a child goes into the fight or flight mode, they either become too active or fidgety. Staying active keeps them maintaining sanity in the mind and prevents tension or frenetic energy.

Other than that, the more laidback and idle we allow our children to be, the more we are risking their chances of gaining weight. Add to that the poor dietary choices and high calorie foods, and we have the perfect recipe on "how to eat to get fat". Ever since the lockdown and pandemic warning, we have stocked up mostly on non-perishables which include frozen foods instead of fresh produce. We have also stocked up on ultra-produced, calorie-dense options instead of picking vegetables and fruits to boost immunity. Also, since we are spending all the time at home, we feel hungrier than ever and are always on the lookout for something to munch on. We have pushed our kids towards bad choices deliberately and then complain about why they feel so lazy and energy-less. Well, news flash, all that they have been eating recently is making them run on low energy yet consume more and more.

But that still doesn't answer as to why do we have to prioritize our fitness when we are already in a survival mode? The answer is simple: we have to!

We can't let our poor dietary choices and poor fitness regimes be the reason why first responders, doctors, and nurses have to work tirelessly and try to save us. It would be selfish not to take care of yourself and then burden them with our presence when our immune system fails to fight back the virus.

If we encourage our kids and motivate ourselves to take up healthy exercising, we may have a chance to beat the virus—even if we contract it. If we equip our body with the right foods that boost immunity and then maintain a healthy and active lifestyle, we may be able to save our families from the grief of losing a loved one.

The Perks of Staying Active

According to WHO, one must spend 150 minutes doing a moderate-intensity workout weekly or 75-minutes of high-intensity workout per week. The recommendations don't suggest the use of any weight-lifting or exercising equipment and can easily be achieved at home.

When data from a health study in Norway was examined consisting of the experiences of approximately 34,000 Norwegian adults following their lives for 11 years, it was revealed that the ones who had an active lifestyle and exercised regularly showed fewer signs of depression and anxiety (Storeng et al., 2018). This was one of the biggest studies and came to be known as the Health Study of

Nord-Trøndelag (HUNT study). The gathered data also looked at even small attempts to exercise and how it protected those individuals against depression. As per the findings, if only the participants had exercised for an hour per week, they would have prevented many symptoms of depression. In fact, 12% of the cases of depression—self-reported by the individuals—could have been prevented.

In another study's review published in the Journal of Sports and Health Science, working out for as little as 60 minutes per week while engaging in moderate to high-intensity workouts, can play a crucial role in boosting one's immunity (Nieman & Wentz, 2019). Additionally, the research also revealed that engaging in a moderate-intensity workout routine surprisingly reduced upper-respiratory infections too and decreased the incidence of fatality from pneumonia or influenza.

Apart from that, there are many other health benefits of exercising and opting for a healthy lifestyle. Knowing these will help you take up exercise yourself as well as convince your children to engage in some too.

Exercise reduces stress and anxiety. Exercise builds resilience. It releases mood-boosting chemicals that help one stay positive and ward off negativity. It makes us feel good about ourselves by releasing the feel-good chemical called dopamine which is the antibody for cortisol.

Exercise also helps us sleep better by improving the quality of sleep. WHO recommends sleeping at least eight hours every night to boost immunity. Additionally, it lowers the risk of cardiovascular diseases as well as lowers blood pressure, ultimately improving our cholesterol profile.

How to Encourage Teenagers to Stay Active

Staying active but indoors? That is something unheard of. Of course, a gym or a fitness center seems like the best place to work out and burn some calories but since it isn't an option currently, we have to make the most of what we have at home. You can always engage the kids to become more active by cutting down the amount of time they spend sitting and browsing Netflix. Not only are they tiring out their eyes, but they are also not doing their bodies any favors. Thus, the best way to ensure that they don't spend most of their days and nights binge-watching their favorite TV shows without moving an inch is to keep them busy with chores. This is what we call sneaking movement into normal routines. Here's how you are going to do it.

Start with dividing chores between yourself and your children. Some will get sweeping, some will be responsible for laundry and some for vacuuming. To guarantee implementation, you can set a certain hour of the day to set up a routine. Household chores like dusting, scrubbing, and cleaning allow children to incorporate some movement into their otherwise sedentary lifestyle and move their legs and muscles.

Other than that, if your kids remain glued to the TV screen all day, you can make it a rule to utilize the time for commercials to do a few squats, lunges, push-ups, or jumping jacks.

There are many other indoor activities that you can engage in together as a team. For example, you all can play your favorite songs, pump up the volume, and get dancing. Aerobics, Zumba, and dancing don't require any treadmills or elliptical machines. You just need some great music and your favorite people to accompany you on the floor and move your body. You don't have to coordinate your moves. You simply have to shake and move enough to get your heart racing.

If you want some calm and peace in the house, you can opt for Pilates or yoga too. Yoga has countless health benefits, a reduction in stress and anxiety being a prominent one (Sharma, 2013).

Take a Virtual Class

Many personal trainers have taken their businesses online by promoting online classes. There are many paid and free to subscribe to and join live exercise sessions with your fitness coaches. The reason it is ideal for you and your children is that it adds an accountability factor. When you have already paid the subscription fee or paid for the course, you are more likely to attend it. Some trainers are also featuring personal training sessions based on personal needs and preferences. Besides, since the overall goal is to find something better and uplifting to do during the pandemic, this will also provide your kids with the opportunity to interact with others in a fun and engaging way.

Go to YouTube for Free Videos

If you are not into the paid subscription thing, you can always ask your teenager to search for videos based on their personal preference. For instance, if your teenage daughter wants to learn belly dancing instead of opting for a high-intensity workout, you can help her come across many online free videos on YouTube or via mobile apps to learn. There isn't a doubt that portals like YouTube offer viewers millions of exercise-related videos to choose from, making it easier for everyone to find something they like.

Go Outside

Based on the guidelines provided by your local public health officials, you can also go out for a run or jog to the park as long as you follow the precautionary measures of maintaining social distancing and keeping yourself and others around you safe by wearing a mask and applying hand sanitizer from time to time. You can add riding bikes to your agenda and motivate your kids to join you. The less traffic on the roads also makes it safer for you and your child to enjoy some fresh air and clean views, all while you exercise. If you are too worried about leaving the house, you and your children can opt for activities like yard work, building a treehouse in the backyard, building a shelter for your pet, or growing fruits and vegetables in the garden. The more sunshine you get, the more vitamin D your body absorbs.

Conclusion

For all we know right now, tougher times are coming. As soon as the pandemic ends, we will be faced with yet another and bigger problem (i.e. stabilizing the economy). The people who have lost jobs during the lockdown, the companies that have gone bankrupt or closed down due to lack of finances will need to restart from scratch again. The competition will only get tougher. Children will need to adapt to the changing demand and supply and make themselves valuable.

It all starts with the right social skills and flexibility. They do not need to be afraid anymore by the challenges that lay ahead; they know how not to give in to anxiety, and feel confident in their skills and talents. They must know how to communicate, behave, and respect others. They need to learn to listen and offer empathy. They must be open to collaboration.

The reason we are telling you this is because this, right now, is the time to train them and prepare them for professional life. Soon, they will head for college life and then into the professional world. They will need these essential skills to land themselves a good and promising job. Since they can no longer rely on their teachers and educators to work with them and train them for the upcoming future, you have to take up that role and ensure that they are their best selves. Use this time to teach them about the importance of time management, stress regulation strategies, and mindfulness so that when they step out of that door, they no longer feel anxiety creeping in. Instead, they must feel confident and ready for the world and all the challenges that lay ahead. Moreover, the busier they are, the more distracted they will be and the less time they will have to themselves to allow loneliness to set in.

Thank you for giving this a read. I hope you loved it too because I certainly enjoyed writing it. It would make me the happiest if you would take a moment to leave an honest review. All you have to do is visit the site from where you purchased it. It's that simple! It doesn't have to be a full-fledged paragraph, just a few words will do too. Your few words will help others decide if this is what they should be reading too. Thank you in advance and best of luck with your parenting excursions. Surely, every moment is a joyous one with a kid.

References

Artley, A. (2020, April). Exercise During
    Coronavirus: Tips for Staying Active -
    HelpGuide.org. Help Guide.
    https://www.helpguide.org/articles/healthy-
    living/exercise-during-coronavirus.htm

Barlow, N. (2018, June 22). It's true-Fake news is
    bad for your health. About Manchester.
    https://aboutmanchester.co.uk/its-true-fake-
    news-is-bad-for-your-health/

Bentley, V. (2020, April 9). How mindfulness can
    help you cope during COVID-19.
    Intermountainhealthcare.Org.
    https://intermountainhealthcare.org/blogs/t
    opics/covid-19/2020/04/how-mindfulness-
    can-help-you-cope-during-covid-19/

Beusekom, M. V. (2020, May 12). Scientists: "Exactly
    zero" evidence COVID-19 came from a lab.
    CIDRAP.
    https://www.cidrap.umn.edu/news-
    perspective/2020/05/scientists-exactly-zero-
    evidence-covid-19-came-lab

BNI Treatment Centers. (2020, March 26). Isolation
    in Teens During Coronavirus. BNI Treatment
    Centers. https://bnitreatment.com/isolation-
    in-teens-during-coronavirus/

Boone, L. (2020, April 29). Teens are feeling lonely and anxious in isolation. Here's how parents can help. Los Angeles Times. https://www.latimes.com/lifestyle/story/2020-04-29/parenting-teens-coronavirus

Branstetter, M. R. (2020, April 7). COVID-19 Stress: Coping Skills for Parents and Children. Youth First. https://youthfirstinc.org/covid-19-stress-coping-skills-for-parents-and-children/

Building Blocks | Creating Structure | Essentials | Parenting Information | CDC. (2020, June 8). Www.Cdc.Gov. https://www.cdc.gov/parents/essentials/structure/building.html

Cherry, K. (2020, March 30). How to Practice Empathy During the COVID-19 Pandemic. Verywell Mind. https://www.verywellmind.com/how-to-practice-empathy-during-the-covid-19-pandemic-4800924

Coping with Coronavirus (COVID-19). (n.d.). Coping Skills for Kids. Retrieved July 3, 2020, from https://copingskillsforkids.com/coping-with-coronavirus

Exercise is Essential for Well-Being During COVID-19 Pandemic. (n.d.). Health Quest Patient Center. https://patients.healthquest.org/exercise-is-essential-for-well-being-during-covid-19-pandemic/

Fegert, J. M., Vitiello, B., Plener, P. L., & Clemens, V. (2020). Challenges and burden of the Coronavirus 2019 (COVID-19) pandemic for child and adolescent mental health: a narrative review to highlight clinical and research needs in the acute phase and the long return to normality. Child and Adolescent Psychiatry and Mental Health, 14(1). https://doi.org/10.1186/s13034-020-00329-3

Goodman, J., & Carmichael, F. (2020, May 30). The Bill Gates 'microchip' claim fact-checked. BBC News. https://www.bbc.com/news/52847648

Jacobson, R. (2020, March 23). How Mindfulness Can Help During COVID-19. Child Mind Institute; Child Mind Institute. https://childmind.org/article/how-mindfulness-can-help-during-covid-19/

Jones, J. K. (2018, December 2). The Benefits of
    Mindfulness Meditation for Teens. World of
    Psychology.
    https://psychcentral.com/blog/the-benefits-
    of-mindfulness-meditation-for-teens/

Kim, C. S. (2020, March 24). Establishing structure
    and routine for kids during COVID-19. CHOC
    Children's Blog.
    https://blog.chocchildrens.org/establishing-
    structure-and-routine-for-kids-during-covid-
    19/

Loades, M. E., Chatburn, E., Higson-Sweeney, N.,
    Reynolds, S., Shafran, R., Brigden, A., Linney,
    C., McManus, M. N., Borwick, C., & Crawley,
    E. (2020). Rapid Systematic Review: The
    Impact of Social Isolation and Loneliness on
    the Mental Health of Children and
    Adolescents in the Context of COVID-19.
    Journal of the American Academy of Child &
    Adolescent Psychiatry.
    https://doi.org/10.1016/j.jaac.2020.05.009

Nieman, D. C., & Wentz, L. M. (2019). The
    compelling link between physical activity and
    the body's defense system. Journal of Sport
    and Health Science, 8(3), 201–217.
    https://doi.org/10.1016/j.jshs.2018.09.009

Sharma, M. (2013). Yoga as an Alternative and Complementary Approach for Stress Management. Journal of Evidence-Based Complementary & Alternative Medicine, 19(1), 59–67. https://doi.org/10.1177/2156587213503344

Shih, G. (2020, March 5). Conspiracy theorists blame U.S. for coronavirus. China is happy to encourage them. Washington Post. https://www.washingtonpost.com/world/asi a_pacific/conspiracy-theorists-blame-the-us-for-coronavirus-china-is-happy-to-encourage-them/2020/03/05/50875458-5dc8-11ea-ac50-18701e14e06d_story.html

Sorbring, E., & Lansford, J. E. (2019). School systems, parent behavior, and academic achievement□: an international perspective. Springer.

Stein, N. (2020, March 25). COVID-19 and Exercise: Staying Active while Socially Distancing. Lark Health. https://www.lark.com/blog/covid-19-and-exercise/

Storeng, S. H., Sund, E. R., & Krokstad, S. (2018). Factors associated with basic and instrumental activities of daily living in elderly participants of a population-based survey: the Nord-Trøndelag Health Study, Norway. BMJ Open, 8(3), e018942. https://doi.org/10.1136/bmjopen-2017-018942

Teens Need to Manage Stress. Parents Are Best-Positioned to Help. (2018, September 4). Center for Parent and Teen Communication. https://parentandteen.com/teaching-teens-coping-skills-one-of-the-7-cs-of-resilience/

Walter, K. (2020, June 2). COVID-19 Lockdown Having an Impact on Adolescent Mental Health. HCPLive®. https://www.mdmag.com/medical-news/covid-19-lockdown-adolescent-mental-health

Why Parents Must Have Empathy for Teens During the COVID-19 Pandemic. (2020, May 6). Center for Parent and Teen Communication. https://parentandteen.com/empathy-covid-19/

Made in the USA
Coppell, TX
23 April 2021